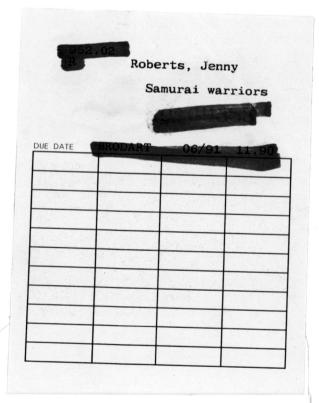

© Aladdin Books Ltd 1990

*First published in
the United States in 1990 by*
Gloucester Press
387 Park Avenue South
New York NY 10016

Printed in Belgium

*Design*    David West
Children's Book Design

*Editor*    Catherine Bradley

*Picture Research*  Cecilia Weston-Baker

*Illustrator*   Tony Smith

*Map*    Aziz Khan

*The author, Jenny Roberts, was a founder-editor of the Rialto Poetry Magazine.*

*The consultant, Stephen Turnbull, is an expert on Medieval Japan. He has written many books on the subject including* Samurai Warriors *and* Samurai Warlords.

Roberts, Jenny.
    Samurai warriors / Jenny Roberts.
        p. cm. -- History highlights
    Summary: Traces the history of Japan's feudal systems and discusses the roles, functions and duties of the samurai warriors.
    ISBN 0-531-17202-3
    1. Samurai--Juvenile literature. [1. Samurai. 2.
Japan--History--1185-1868.] I. Title. II. Series: History highlights New York, N.Y.)
DS827.S3R63 1990
952'.02--dc20          89   26020          CIP AC

# Contents

# HISTORY HIGHLIGHTS

# SAMURAI WARRIORS

# GLOUCESTER PRESS

**London · New York · Toronto · Sydney**

# INTRODUCTION

The *samurai* were Japanese knights, rather like the knights of the Middle Ages in Europe. Today Japan is a rich, powerful and highly industrialized country. However, at the time of the *samurai* it was a collection of islands off China's coast, whose people lived by fishing and farming. Japan has been greatly influenced by China, whose civilization from the 7th to the 14th century was very advanced. China was ruled by an emperor who had officials to help him run the country.

4

Japan had its first emperor in about AD 400. Gradually it developed a system where the emperor and his chief general, called the *shogun*, were at the top. Next came the *daimyos*, who were important landowners. Below the *daimyo* came the *samurai*, who fought on his behalf. Beneath the *samurai* were the farmers, then the craftsmen. Merchants and peasants were at the bottom. Each class had to obey the class above it. This system is known as the feudal system and it also existed in Europe. In the 12th century the emperors lost control of Japan and clans supported by armies of *samurai* warriors fought against each other.

**A Japanese garden shows the qualities which Japanese people value: grace and harmony. The arts have always flourished in Japan. Japanese people love beauty and perfection. Their pottery, paintings, temples and gardens are exquisite.**

## JAPAN

Japan is a small country set on a group of islands in Far East Asia. It has a very large population for its size and its main food crop is rice. The climate of Japan is temperate and there are orchards of plum and cherry trees. It has some very large cities full of sky-scrapers, as well as mountains and forests. The capital of Japan is Tokyo. It has over eight million inhabitants. After its defeat in the Second World War, Japan had to rebuild its industry. It is now a leading manufacturer of goods.

KOREA

HOKKAIDO

SEA OF JAPAN

HONSHU

KYUSHU

SKIKOKU

PACIFIC OCEAN

# WHO WERE THE *SAMURAI* ?

The *samurai* were the warriors of Japan from the 12th century until the founding of modern Japan in the mid-19th century. In the same way as medieval knights of Europe valued their honor above all things, so too did the *samurai*. They called their code of honor *bushido* which means "the way of the warrior." The *samurai* believed that they had to obey their master; this allegiance came before anything else like friendship or family ties.

A *samurai* was supposed to be always alert and ready to do battle on his lord's behalf. He was prepared to give his life in his master's service. A *samurai* would always rush into the fiercest fighting, eager for glory. He would not retreat unless ordered to do so, and would never allow himself to be taken prisoner.

The way of the *samurai* demanded perfection in matters of honor, both on the battlefield and in daily life. A *samurai* was also expected to be able to write, understand poetry and perform traditional dances.

# RITUAL *SEPPUKU* SWORD

Sometimes a *samurai* would take his own life if he felt he had behaved dishonorably. This was done by cutting his own stomach open in a ritual known as *seppuku*; this is often (and incorrectly) known as *hara-kiri*. When this was done, a friend would quickly cut off his head with a specially sharpened sword. A *samurai* would also commit suicide if he was in danger of being captured or if his master had given him an order that went against his conscience.

Seppuku swords were very beautifully made. The hilt of the sword was often covered in fishskin. The scabbard was also richly decorated with lacquer, jewels and precious metals. The craftsmen who made these swords were highly regarded.

All *samurai* were trained in archery and sword-fighting. They were brilliant horsemen and took good care of their horses. The *samurai* were also expert at unarmed fighting like *jujutsu*.

# ARMS AND ARMOR

*Samurai* swords were the finest ever made anywhere in the world. The *samurai* usually had both a long and a short sword. The *wakizashi* was a short sword and was worn at the waist. A longer curved sword called the *katana* was thrust through the belt. As well as these, a samurai often carried a *naginata* which is a long pole with a curved blade at the end.

The *samurai* wore special suits of armor made by craftsmen. These craftsmen also made the swords and were greatly respected by the *samurai*. The quality of the work was very high. Not only were the arms and armor of the *samurai* skilfully made, they were also extremely decorative. Swords were thought to be so important that special mystic rituals were performed while they were being made.

Early *samurai* warriors were mounted archers and carried longbows and arrows into battle. No armor was worn on the right arm to allow the warrior to draw his bowstring back.

A *samurai* would have a metal helmet with special flaps to protect the neck. Warriors often wore beautifully decorated helmets and fierce-looking face masks to frighten their enemies.

*Samurai* armor was constructed from separate plates bound together with silk or leather thongs. It was all in one piece like a box, and fastened around the waist. Only the section under the right arm was separate. This was known as a *yoroi*.

# KAMIKAZE

In 1274 Japan was threatened with invasion by the Mongol forces of China under the emperor Kublai Khan. He had already conquered most of Eastern Europe and Asia. The Mongols had prepared a large fleet of ships and at first they seemed to be winning as they were better organized. But when night fell there was an enormous storm which forced the Mongol troops away from Japan and back out to sea. Eventually, with 13,000 men drowned, the Mongols retreated to China.

In 1281 the Mongols again prepared to invade Japan, with an even larger force. This time the *samurai* were better prepared and had a fleet of their own. They fought with the Mongols in the Bay of Hakata. After two months a typhoon again helped to defeat the Mongols with even greater losses than before.

After this the Japanese believed that the strong winds which had twice saved them from the Mongols were sent from the gods. They were called *kamikaze* which means "divine winds."

Despite being unprepared for an invasion, the *samurai* were able to fight off the Mongols in 1274. After the first invasion, the Japanese built great walls to defend themselves from future attacks. Kublai Khan went on planning to conquer Japan until his death in 1294.

## *Kamikaze* pilots

In World War II, many young Japanese pilots were taught to believe they were the "divine winds." The *kamikaze* pilots would die crashing their aircraft into American warships. They would sometimes whiten their faces as the *samurai* had done. They often wore red headbands and white clothes as a sign of ritual purification. The aircraft were packed with explosives. As the young pilots climbed aboard they would say "see you at Yasukini," meaning that their spirits would meet again at this famous Shinto shrine. Their sacrifice was a useless gesture and made no difference to the war's outcome.

# *SAMURAI* RELIGION

Shinto was the first religion of the Japanese people. Followers of Shinto believe that all natural objects contain a god. They also believe that the first emperor of Japan was a descendant of the Sun Goddess, so they think of their emperor as a god.

The followers of Shinto built many shrines because they thought that the spirits of the dead used them as gathering places. At certain times in the year, people light lanterns and float them on the water to light the path for the spirits as they return to their home in the mountains.

Buddhism was introduced to Japan from China. The *samurai* believed in a kind of Buddhism known as Zen. The word Zen means meditation or focusing the mind on a single object or idea. Believers in Zen think that they can find truth and knowledge through meditation and self-control. The *samurai* thought that Zen would help them act without hesitation, especially in battle, and develop inner peace.

**The most famous statue of Buddha is at Kamakura. It is made of bronze and was created in 1252. Originally it was surrounded by a wooden temple, but this was swept away by a giant tidal wave in 1495.**

## THE ISE SHRINE

The most holy Shinto shrine in Japan is the Ise shrine. It is rebuilt every 20 years. Two sacred treasures – a jewel and a mirror – are kept there. The Sun Goddess is believed to have given these things to the first Japanese emperor, Jimmu. The shrine is based on the design of a prehistoric grindstone. It was last rebuilt in 1973.

# THE ARTS

*Samurai* were not just skilful warriors. They were expected to understand and appreciate all forms of art. The *samurai* enjoyed reciting and composing poetry. In the middle of the 17th century the poet Matsuo Basho developed the *haiku*, a 17-syllable poem in praise of nature. The *samurai* would have written these and read them to one another.

The *samurai* also learned the traditional forms of dancing. The fierce General Oda Nobunaga is said to have danced gracefully with a fan in front of his troops before leading them into battle.

The *samurai* enjoyed theater. In the 12th century they attended popular plays known as *kabuki*. Toward the end of the *samurai* period, the classical Japanese theater of *Noh* was considered more suitable. In both kinds of theater, the women's parts were played by boys. "Practice the arts of peace on the left hand, and the arts of war on the right" was a popular *samurai* saying of the time.

The *samurai* appreciated calligraphy, which is the art of writing with brush and ink on paper. Each "character" has to be painted gracefully and accurately, without hesitation.

## SASHIMONO

*Samurai* warriors had a *sashimono*, or personal flag, which was worn on the back in a special carrier. These identified the wearer and often had a poem written on them. In the case of one clan, the *sashimono* of the whole army would spell out a longer poem when everyone was together. It said: "Colors are fragrant, but they fade away. In this world of ours none lasts forever. Today cross the high mountains of life's illusion, and there will be no more dreaming, no more drunkenness."

# SAMURAI WOMEN

*Samurai* women followed the same code of honor as the men. They were expected to show the same obedience to their fathers and husbands as a *samurai* would to his master. Women were often forced into arranged marriages in order to increase the power of their families.

It was considered very important that a *samurai* had a son to inherit his possessions. Sometimes the *samurai* would take another wife if the first one did not give birth to a boy.

**One *samurai* woman, Tomoe Gozen, fought alongside her husband, Yoshinaka, in all his battles. Her story is told in the long poem *Heike Monogotari*.**

Some *samurai* women learned to fight and they defended their homes against enemies; in defeat, they also committed *seppuku*. One *kabuki* play tells of two sisters, Miyagino and Shinobu, whose father was murdered by a *samurai* called Shiga. They swore to avenge their father's death. In secret they trained themselves to fight, then they went to the local *daimyo* and asked permission to challenge Shiga to a duel. In the fight that followed, Shiga was killed and family honor was satisfied. The story of Miyagino and Shinobu is still performed on the Japanese stage to this day. It shows the courage of *samurai* women.

## *SAMURAI* CHILDREN

In the Edo period, schools were set up for the sons of *samurai*. Calligraphy and Chinese writings were the main subjects taught, as well as the *samurai* codes. Girls learned *ikebana*, the art of flower arranging, and the tea ceremony from their mothers. At the age of 13, boys had the front part of their heads shaved. This was a sign that they had become men.

Girls wore their hair parted in the middle and falling over their shoulders. By the time they grew up, it touched the ground. Boys liked to catch dragonflies and make them fight each other. Girls caught fireflies and kept them in jars to use as lanterns.

13 year-old boy

Young boy

Young girl

# THE EMPEROR AND HIS COURT

Although the emperor of Japan was considered to be a living god, most emperors did not have much say in how the country was run. Various powerful families would marry their daughters into the imperial family and gain control over national affairs.

Until the 12th century the court was based at Kyoto, and the Fujiwara family dominated court life. The emperors would ascend to the throne while they were children and then abdicate before they grew up. The Fujiwara family would act as regents to these child emperors, and tell them what to do.

In the 12th century many of the emperors became priests and were known as "cloistered" emperors. In any case, much of their time was taken up with religious duties and rituals. The court was later established at Kamakura, and the real power passed to the *shogun* who commanded the *samurai*.

A favorite pastime of the emperor and his court was watching *Noh* plays, which told tales from ancient Japanese legends. Delightful entertainments, plays and concerts were arranged at court. It became an artificial world devoted to beauty, poetry and the pursuits of perfection.

## COURT LADIES

Japanese courtiers were very well educated. Lady Murasaku wrote a story called *The Tale of Genji* about the exploits of a prince. Very rich ladies had nothing to do, and so made themselves look beautiful. It was fashionable to have white faces, red cheeks and blackened teeth. This is an 18th century print of a *geisha* and her client. During the late *samurai* age, especially intelligent and educated women called *geishas* provided rich men with interesting company. The word *geisha* means "art person." Even today, *geishas* act as hostesses at business meetings.

# SHOGUNS AND DAIMYOS

In the 12th century two powerful clans, the Minamoto and the Taira, declared war on each other. Minamoto Yoritomo won and he forced the emperor to give him the title of *shogun*, which means "commander-in-chief for the suppression of barbarians." He ruled Japan through his officials called *shugos*. Their job was to collect taxes and keep order. Taxes were paid in *koku* of rice. One *koku* was equal to the amount of rice that one man would eat in a year. The more land a *samurai* had, the more *koku* of rice he had to pay.

## *DAIMYOS* AND CULTURE

This print shows a *daimyo* sitting on a battlefield. To show their importance, *daimyos* liked to surround themselves with beautiful things. They often commissioned hand-painted screens and ceramics for their castles. A *daimyo* thought that performing the tea ceremony or looking at a landscaped garden were just as important as making war. When they went into battle, the *daimyos* took pride in the beauty of their intricate armor.

20

A *daimyo* visits the *shogun*. Before setting out for battle, the *daimyo* would eat a ritual meal of dried chestnuts, seaweed and abalone. He would drink rice wine served within three cups, one inside the other. These things were thought to bring good luck.

With time, nobles began to resent the *shogun*. They wanted more power in their own regions. Rich people built castles and called themselves *daimyo*, which means "big name." The *daimyos* recruited many loyal *samurai* and fought with other *daimyos*. They did not always obey the *shogun*. In 1603 a *shogun* called Tokugawa Ieyasu found a way of controlling the *daimyos*. He forced the *daimyo* wives and children to live at Edo, now known as Tokyo. The *daimyos* were only allowed to live there every other year. The rest of the time they lived at their castles. The *shogun* could hold a *daimyo* family as hostages if the *daimyo* rebelled.

21

# *SAMURAI* BATTLES

Before a battle could begin, messengers were sent from each side to decide when and where the battle would take place. When this was agreed, the two armies would draw up facing each other. One *samurai* from each side would step forward and would shout out the reason they were fighting. Then two "humming" arrows were fired in the air, which was a signal for the fighting to start. Mounted *samurai* on each side would fire their arrows into the enemy, then they would charge and begin their attack.

It was important to find someone of the same rank to fight. The *samurai* would try to knock each other from their horses. Then they would fight hand to hand on the ground until one of them was dead.

The *samurai* were rewarded by their masters if they fought well. They were given land and money. The *samurai* would cut the heads off their victims, and a servant would collect them up and bring them home. The *samurai* were rewarded according to how important their opponents had been.

Armies were controlled on the battlefield by big war-drums called *taiko* and by blowing conch shells known as *horagai*. An expert could blow the *horagai* loud enough to be heard six miles away. *Horagai* were also used to tell the soldiers what time it was.

## CASTLES

*Daimyos* often built fortresses to defend themselves from their enemies. These would be built wherever there were natural defenses like hilltops, and were made of wood. Later castles were built of stone on an earth mound; they were solidly built to withstand earthquakes. The most beautiful example of these is Inuyama castle.

# THREE GREAT LEADERS

During the 16th and 17th centuries three great leaders came to power. The first was Oda Nobunaga. After his victory at the Battle of Okehazama he made peace with his enemies by arranging marriages between them and women in his family. Oda Nobunaga established a strong army and chose his generals well. He also abolished the post of *shogun* but was eventually defeated in battle. Toyotomi Hideyoshi succeeded Nobunaga and was able to unify Japan. He brought the islands of Shikoku and Kyushu into Japan. By 1590 all of Japan had yielded to Hideyoshi except for the Hojo clan. Eventually even they submitted.

When Hideyoshi died leaving only an infant heir, Tokugawa Ieyasu took over. He made the position of *shogun* strong once again. He also founded a new capital at Edo, present-day Tokyo. Any *daimyo* who was not loyal was sent as far away from Edo as possible. Under the rule of Tokugawa Ieyasu, Japan became one nation at last.

**Toyotomi Hideyoshi
1539-1598**
He started life as an *ashigaru*, or foot soldier, in Nobunaga's army and soon rose to the rank of general. Toyotomi Hideyoshi twice tried to invade Korea, but failed.

**Oda Nobunaga 1535-1582**
He came from a humble family and had a reputation for being very cunning. After his defeat in battle he committed *seppuku* in the temple where he was hiding.

**Tokugawa Ieyasu 1542-1616**
As he was from the Minamoto clan, he took the title of *shogun* and established the Tokugawa Shogunate. He had a network of spies who told him if any *daimyo* rebelled.

# WHAT HAPPENED TO THE *SAMURAI*?

After Japan had been united by Tokugawa Ieyasu, the *samurai* were rarely needed to fight battles. The *daimyos* became poorer as they were forced to pay for repairs on the *shogun's* castles. They could no longer afford to support huge armies.

First Portuguese and then Dutch traders came to Japan, and merchants and traders grew richer and more important. Although some *shoguns* tried to stop too many traders from coming to Japan, the old way of life was changing. The *samurai* became warriors without a war to fight.

Some *samurai* became craftsmen; some became teachers or worked for the government. The sword makers and armor builders lost their living and instead made pots and pans. One of the last deeds of the *samurai* was to overthrow the shogunate, and to put the emperor back on the throne in 1867. Finally, in the 1870s, the *samurai* class was abolished and they lost their special rights like wearing swords.

**In 1853 four American ships arrived in Japan under Commodore Perry. Trade treaties were signed with Britain, the United States and Russia. The Japanese began to copy Western habits and to wear Western clothes.**

## THE FORTY-SEVEN RONIN

In 1701 a *daimyo* called Asano was executed and his land confiscated. His *samurai* became *ronin*, meaning they had no master. Some 47 of these *ronin* ki¹led the man responsible for Asano's death. Such acts of revenge were by then illegal, so they were forced to commit suicide.

# *SAMURAI* TODAY

Today Japan is a rich and modern country. Japan exports goods like cars, electronics and machinery all over the world.

However, there are many aspects of Japanese life that remind us of the age of the *samurai*. The arts are still considered to be very important. Examples of calligraphy, ceramics and paintings are found in most Japanese homes. Women still perform the tea ceremony at home or in special tea houses where businessmen come to relax after a busy day.

Although many people still enjoy Western entertainment, the traditional sports of kendo, judo and karate are still very popular. On television people still watch *kabuki* plays and *Noh* dramas.

Many customs still reflect the ways of *samurai*. Japanese children obey their parents and work hard at school. Japanese workers are very loyal to the company that employs them; in return the company looks after the work force and provides training and cheap housing. This loyalty to the company is rather like the loyalty that a *samurai* would have shown to his lord.

The tea ceremony is a traditional ritual for sharing tea with friends. Tea is served in delicate china bowls and there is always a graceful flower arrangement in a special vase. Japanese people appreciate the harmony and tranquillity of this simple act and it is an important part of Japanese culture.

## THE SEVEN *SAMURAI*

Many writers and film directors have been inspired by the *samurai* legends. In 1956 the Japanese film director Akira Kurosawa made a film called *The Seven Samurai*. It won international awards and is still a great favorite with Japanese and Western audiences. It is the story of seven *ronin*, who band together to defend a village against bandits. Each *samurai* is master of a different combat skill, and they drive off the bandits with brilliant fighting and clever strategy. In 1960 John Sturges remade the film as a Western, called *The Magnificent Seven*.

# DATE CHARTS

**AD 794** Heian period begins

**858** Fujiwara family gains power

**1010** Lady Murasaki writes *The Tale of Genji*

**1180-85** The Gempei war between the Minamoto and the Taira clan; the Minamoto win

**1183** Tomoe Gozen fights in battle of Kurikara alongside her husband Minamoto Yoshinaka

**1191** The monk Eisai visits China and brings back Zen Buddhism

**1192** Kamakura Shogunate established by Minamoto Yoritomo

**1240** First great war epic: *Heike Monogotari*

**1274** The First Mongol Invasion

**1281** The Second Mongol Invasion

**1338** Ashikaga Shogunate established

**1467-1603** The age of strife; many small wars fought before unification

**1543** The Portuguese arrive in Japan, bringing guns

**1549** St Francis Xavier spreads Christianity in Japan

**1568** Oda Nobunaga takes power from shogunate; begins to unify Japan

**1584** Toyotomi Hideyoshi controls Japan

**1592** Hideyoshi fails to invade Korea

**1597** Second invasion of Korea

**1603** Tokugawa Ieyasu becomes *shogun*. He establishes new capital at Edo

**1616** Christianity abolished. Japan tries to discourage foreign influence

**1702** The 47 *Ronin* are punished for avenging their master's death in traditional *samurai* style

**1774** First translation of foreign books into Japanese

**1853** Commodore Perry arrives in Japan from America

**1868** Shogunate rule abolished. Emperor Meiji restored to power

**1870** Special rights of *samurai* abolished

**1876** Swords banned

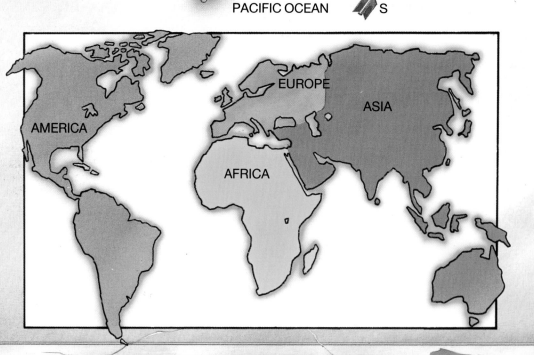

30

| AFRICA | ASIA | AMERICA | EUROPE |
|---|---|---|---|
| | **c1010 AD** Lady Murasaki writes *Tale of Genji*<br>**1031** Jain Temple built on Mount Abu, India | | **1016 AD** Canute ascends English throne |
| **1070 AD** Constantine the African translates Greek medical texts into Latin, bringing medicine to West | | | **1066** William of Normandy invades Britain |
| | | | **1086** Domesday book finished in England |
| **1173** Saladin assumes power in Egypt | | | **1170** Death of Thomas à Becket |
| | **1180** Gempei war in Japan | | |
| | **1192** Kamakura Shogunate in Japan | **1200 AD** Inca rule established in Peru | **1215** King John signs the Magna Carta |
| | **1271** Marco Polo reached China | | |
| | **1338** Ashikaga Shogunate in Japan | | **1340** Black Death reaches Europe |
| **1352** Ib Battuta crosses Sahara Desert | | | **1381** Peasants' revolt in England |
| | **1421** Beijing established as capital of China | **1492** Christopher Columbus sails to America | |
| **1505** Mozambique founded | | **1519** Cortes defeats Aztecs | |
| | **1526** Mogul Empire of India founded<br>**1545** Portuguese arrive in Japan | | |
| | **1603** Tokugawa Shogunate in Japan | | **1558** Queen Elizabeth I ascends English throne |
| **1652** Capetown founded in South Africa | | **1776** American Declaration of Independence | |
| | | **1789** George Washington elected President | **1789** French Revolution |
| | | | **1804** Napoleon Bonaparte declared Emperor of France |
| | | | **1837** Queen Victoria ascends English throne |
| | **1868** Emperor Meiji restored to power in Japan<br>**1870** *Samurai* privileges abolished | **1853** Commodore Perry arrives in Japan | **1870** Franco-Prussian War |

# INDEX

Photographic credits:
Pages 7, 19, 27 and back cover: Werner Forman Archive; page 10; Popperfoto; page 12: Japanese Information Center; Pages 20 and 23: Eastern Images; page 28: British Film Institute.